GRANDPARENTING *for Beginners*

GRANDPARENTING

for Beginners

CLIVE WHICHELOW

summersdale

GRANDPARENTING FOR BEGINNERS

Summersdale Publishers Ltd
46 West Street
Chichester
West Sussex
PO19 1RP
UK

www.summersdale.com

Printed and bound in China

ISBN: 978-1-84953-753-7

Substantial discounts on bulk quantities of Summersdale books are available to corporations, professional associations and other organisations. For details contact Nicky Douglas by telephone: +44 (0) 1243 756902, fax: +44 (0) 1243 786300 or email: nicky@summersdale.com.

INTRODUCTION

The world is full of books for new parents, but what about the poor old grandparents? They hardly get any guidance at all – and boy do they need it!

There you are, kids finally off your hands and fending for themselves… You knew it was too quiet, didn't you? You knew it was too good to be true – yes, your peace and quiet is about to be shattered all over again.

And the trouble is that everything you ever knew about babies has been forgotten. It may have been only twenty or thirty years ago, but you're now about as familiar with the needs of a baby as you are with the needs of a Mongolian yak. In fact, given the choice, you might even prefer the custody of a Mongolian yak – at least you could leave it in the garden overnight.

That may not go down so well if you did it with your dear little grandchild – however noisy they were. You'd be getting a call from social services before you could say 'nappy rash'.

Oh yes, the world has changed since you had little ones of your own – you may now have to read bedtime stories from an e-book, buy designer babygrows and whisk them off to Greenland instead of your local department store to see Father Christmas. Then there are the food allergies, politically correct nativity plays, playground politics and party-bag competitiveness… welcome to grandparenting twenty-first-century style!

WHAT ARE THE BASICS?

A baby has two ends

Food goes in one end and comes
out of the other end

You will need to keep an eye on both

End of lesson one

WHAT IS THE ROLE OF THE GRANDPARENT?

Your job is to spoil them rotten

To allow them everything you denied your own children (i.e. their parents)

To have free licence to enjoy life as much as the grandchildren do

Grandparenting, then, is power without responsibility. E-numbers? Bring 'em on!

WHAT HAS CHANGED SINCE I WAS A PARENT?

Everything

It's just as well you've forgotten everything from first time round because none of it applies any more

You're just like a new parent really – muddling through without a clue about what you're doing

Good luck with that, then!

WHAT ARE THE HOURS?

To ask an older person to be available 24/7 would be completely unreasonable – so now you know just how unreasonable your children are!

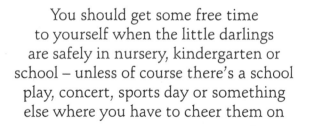

You should get some free time to yourself when the little darlings are safely in nursery, kindergarten or school – unless of course there's a school play, concert, sports day or something else where you have to cheer them on

DOS AND DON'TS

DO

Feel free to occasionally turn down
a request for babysitting

DON'T

Barricade your front door and
put armed guards outside

DO

Ring the parents if you're not
sure about anything

DON'T

Ring the parents to double-check how
many kids they left with you earlier

DO

Give the parents some gentle,
wise advice if necessary

DON'T

Hold up Olympic-style scorecards
after everything they do

WON'T I GET TIRED?

Of course. This is why grandparents
usually come in twos – so one can go and
have a little lie-down now and then

Tired isn't the word for it. Shattered
might be better. Or exhausted, drained,
whacked out – or possibly all three at once

But it's amazing how you'll perk
up when you've kissed the kids
goodbye and your other half utters
the magic words 'glass of wine?'

DO I NEED TO ADAPT ANYTHING AROUND THE HOUSE?

A childproof lock on the drinks cabinet may be advisable – it will also keep your other half out of temptation's way

Create a nice quiet area somewhere – and retreat to it as often as possible

Throw away all your TV and computer instruction manuals – any child over six months old will be able to work your electronic devices better than you can

WILL ALL MY CHILD-REARING SKILLS COME BACK TO ME?

No. They were excised from your memory the moment you vowed never to have any more children

Don't bother asking the new parents – they'll know even less than you do

WHAT WILL YOUR GRANDCHILDREN CALL YOU?

As babies – Something along the lines of 'gaga', 'goo goo', etc.

As children – Grandma, Grandad, Nan, Nana, Nanny, Gramps, etc.

As teenagers – You'll be lucky if they call you at all!

THINGS GRAND-CHILDREN EXPECT GRANDPARENTS TO REMEMBER

Rationing

The reign of Henry VIII

The Gunpowder Plot

Rampaging dinosaurs

WILL YOU BE A GOOD GRANDPARENT OR A BAD GRANDPARENT?

GOOD

You play hide-and-seek with them

BAD

You delay finding them until going-home time

GOOD

You let them do some messy painting

BAD

You make them do all your redecorating

GOOD

You take them out somewhere
nice occasionally

BAD

You let them take you somewhere
nice occasionally

GOOD

You let them help you with some baking

BAD

You get them to cook dinner
while you put your feet up

THINGS NAUGHTY GRANDCHILDREN MAY DO TO WIND YOU UP

Tell you their parents allow them
to have sweets after every meal

Threaten to phone ChildLine
if you tell them off

Refuse to go in the high chair,
saying they suffer from vertigo

Say they need the toilet the moment
you drive on to a motorway

THINGS YOU SHOULD NO LONGER WEAR AS A GRANDPARENT

Studded biker jackets emblazoned with your Hells Angels chapter insignia

Miniskirts (especially you grandads)

Zoo animal onesies – at least not when taking them shopping

Low-slung ripped jeans – assuming you can still get into yours!

THINGS YOU SHOULD NO LONGER SAY AS A GRANDPARENT

Yo!

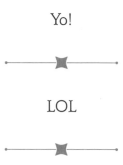

LOL

I'm just off to see my probation officer

Take no notice of me, I'm drunk

HOW YOU MAY INTERPRET WHAT YOUR GRANDCHILDREN SAY

WHAT THEY SAY

I want to go home

YOUR INTERPRETATION

I thought they'd enjoy the Parliament channel

WHAT THEY SAY

I feel sick

YOUR
INTERPRETATION

Perhaps the bouncing on the knee
should have been *before* lunch

WHAT THEY SAY

I love coming to your house

YOUR INTERPRETATION

Maybe I've been overdoing the ice cream, sweets and biscuits

WHAT THEY SAY

Mum and Dad let me do it

YOUR
INTERPRETATION

Mum and Dad would be absolutely
horrified if they found out

HOW TO SPOT ANOTHER GRANDPARENT

At the park they sit and watch instead of joining in anything too energetic

Their grey hair is stuck together with baby food

They seem to actually rather enjoy taking children out

When the children ask for an ice cream/ cola/sweets they actually buy it for them

MODERN NURSERY RHYMES FOR MODERN GRANDPARENTS

Incy wincy spider is now an endangered species

There was an old lady who lived in a shoe but the local authority still found a council tax band for her

The wheels on the bus go round and round extremely slowly in the rush hour

Half a pound of tuppenny rice, half a pound of treacle – you're having a laugh, Grandma, where's the Angel Delight?

HOW THE PARENTS MAY TRANSLATE WHAT YOU SAY

They were as good as gold = At least we stopped short of calling the emergency services

They had their moments = We only had to call one of the emergency services

They were pretty lively = The house has been cordoned off by the police

To be honest, they were quite a handful = We are never, ever babysitting for you again

THINGS YOUR GRANDCHILDREN MAY NOT FIND AS INTERESTING AS YOU DO

Visiting your local history museum

Walking round the garden and finding
out the Latin names of all the plants

Watching *Mastermind*

Listening to CDs of the hits of your youth

THINGS YOUR OWN GRANDPARENTS NEVER HAD TO GO THROUGH

Being frightened out of their wits on white-knuckle theme park rides

Trying to work the computer to see the grandchildren's holiday photos

Having to tell the grandchildren their dinner may contain nuts

Having to buy hugely expensive framed school photos

WAYS IN WHICH OTHER GRANDPARENTS MAY GET COMPETITIVE

YOUR EFFORTS

Taking grandchildren to see Father Christmas in your local department store

---

THEIR EFFORTS

Flying them off to Greenland to see him 'at home'

YOUR EFFORTS

Taking them to the local park

THEIR EFFORTS

Flying them off to Disney World, Florida

YOUR EFFORTS

Letting them pitch a tent
in your back garden

THEIR EFFORTS

Arranging a survival weekend
with Bear Grylls

THINGS YOU THOUGHT YOU'D NEVER HAVE TO DO AGAIN

Change nappies – what, they need changing more than once a day‽!

Tell them to eat their greens – despite not having a clue what rocket or samphire are

Read bedtime stories – and Rupert Bear doesn't look a day older!

Play 'This Little Piggy Went to Market' – in fact, you haven't seen your own toes for quite some time

TIMES WHEN YOU WILL HAVE TO DRAW THE LINE

ACCEPTABLE

Looking after the kids while Mum and Dad go out for a meal

UNACCEPTABLE

Looking after the kids while Mum and Dad have a fortnight in the Seychelles

ACCEPTABLE

Picking the kids up from
school occasionally

UNACCEPTABLE

Being on first-name terms with
all the teachers and the janitor
who think you're the parents

ACCEPTABLE

Helping out financially once in a while

UNACCEPTABLE

Putting the grandchildren through private schools and picking up the tab for their university fees as well

ACCEPTABLE
Having the grandchildren over for tea

UNACCEPTABLE
Hosting their birthday tea with 40 guests

THINGS YOU MAY NOW HAVE AROUND THE HOUSE THAT YOU DIDN'T BEFORE

A high chair

A potty

High-blood-pressure tablets

Quite a lot of broken ornaments

WHAT TO DO IF IT ALL GETS TOO MUCH

Plead temporary insanity and disappear for a few days

Invent a rare medical condition that makes you allergic to small children

Say you've done some family history research and found that, believe it or not, you're not actually related to them

Hire a nanny

WISDOM YOU MAY FIND YOURSELF HANDING OUT TO THE PARENTS

Well, we didn't do it like that in my day!

It's probably just a phase

Before you know it they'll be leaving home

I'm not one to judge, but…

THINGS YOU SHOULD AND SHOULDN'T DO

SHOULD DO

Play games with your grandchildren

SHOULDN'T DO

Try to teach them three-dimensional chess

SHOULD DO

Kiss them better when they
hurt themselves

SHOULDN'T DO

Rush them off to A & E every
time they graze their knees

SHOULD DO
Treat them occasionally

SHOULDN'T DO
Fill them with so much sugar
they levitate off the ground

SHOULD DO
Join in their world of make-believe

SHOULDN'T DO
Actually start believing in it all yourself

WHY GRANDPARENTING IS BETTER THAN PARENTING

You get to sleep right through
every night (unless the little dears
are staying over, of course)

When the grandchildren are older they will
blame the parents for everything, not you

You can always plead old age and frailty

The hours are better

GREAT THINGS YOU CAN NOW **ENJOY**

Watching all those wonderful
kids' TV programmes

Having a share of their sweets, potato
smiley faces and birthday cakes

Playing snap, snakes and ladders,
and blind man's buff

At last, someone thinks you're
absolutely wonderful

NOT SO GREAT THINGS ABOUT BEING A GRANDPARENT

'Grandparent' just sounds
so old, doesn't it?

Just when you were getting
used to a nice quiet life…

In another twenty years you could be a
great-grandparent. How scary is that?

Your lovely, clean, pristine house is
about to get wrecked. Regularly

THINGS ALL GRANDPARENTS MUST HAVE IN THEIR HOUSE BY LAW

A large tin of biscuits

A large tin of sweets

A dressing-up box of old
clothes and jewellery

Something satisfyingly breakable

THE COMPANY
YOU'RE NOW IN

Sir Paul McCartney – a
grandparent since 1999

Goldie Hawn – a grandparent since 2004

Sir Mick Jagger – a grandparent since 1992

Tina Turner – a grandparent since 1985

Donny Osmond – a grandparent
since 2005 (yes, shocking, isn't it?)

Jane Fonda – a grandparent since 1999

CINEMA CLASSIFICATIONS – A GRANDPARENTS' GUIDE

U certificate means even small children should be able to watch the film

PG means some scenes may be unsuitable for little ones

12A means even you might be shocked by some of the language

15 means more sex, violence and swearing than you ever saw in any X film in your day

INSIDE THE CINEMA

Always sit on the end of a row so it's
easy to get to the toilet (that's for your
benefit, by the way, not the kids')

Popcorn comes in three sizes: 'huge',
'ginormous' and 'wheelie bin'

Likewise with the fizzy drinks – which is
why you need to sit at the end of the row

Grab the opportunity for a cheeky nap
when you put on those 3D glasses

THEME PARKS – A GRANDPARENTS' GUIDE

There are two types of theme park: expensive, and flippin' expensive

Avoid any ride that includes the words 'black', 'dragon', 'death' or 'at your own risk'

Take a packed lunch or you'll spend a week's pension/wages on burgers, chips and fizzy drinks

You may be expected to buy a 'fast-track' ticket – basically, legalised queue-jumping

HOW TO BE JUST LIKE YOUR OWN GRANDPARENTS

Smell either of lavender or pipe tobacco

Have white hair – or no hair at all

At least one part of your body should be giving you 'a bit of gyp'

Be totally confused by all modern 'gadgets' (that bit should be easy!)

WAYS IN WHICH GRANDCHILDREN CAN BE AMUSED CHEAPLY

Regale them with stories about how naughty their parents were when they were children

Offer a small cash prize for who can stay quiet the longest

Do some home baking (though this could be offset by extensive cleaning bills)

Long, free bus rides – only if you have your free travel pass already

THINGS CHILDREN EXPECT OF THEIR GRANDPARENTS

First-hand knowledge of 'the olden days' – i.e. everything from the Battle of Hastings to the Moon Landing

Endless supplies of goodies and treats

You won't tell their parents about everything they have been up to behind their backs

Lots of corny jokes and magic tricks with matches and coins

THINGS THEY WON'T EXPECT OF YOU

They know that you will be absolutely useless at any game involving bending down or rolling around on the floor

They won't ask for your advice on how to fix their mobile phone/iPod/iPad

They won't ask for help with their maths homework because you do it 'the old-fashioned way'

They won't ask you to swing them around in the air 'like Daddy does'

WAYS IN WHICH VISITORS WILL BE ABLE TO TELL YOU'RE A GRANDPARENT

School photos on the mantelpiece

Food stains on the carpet

Bits of Lego down the back of the sofa

Tiny fingerprints on the walls

Large felt-tip-pen doodles on the walls

THINGS YOU'LL HAVE TO REMEMBER HOW TO DO AGAIN

Make a paper aeroplane

Play hangman

Make a cat's cradle

Have endless reserves of patience

ZOO TRIPS –
A GRANDPARENTS'
GUIDE

Be careful – these days you may unwittingly
'adopt' an orangutan or a pygmy hippo

You may find the zoo now has
expensive fairground-style rides

In fact, to be honest, now some zoos
are really just theme parks with a
few token animals chucked in

All zoos now have a shop at the
exit to fleece you of your last few
quid just before going home

CHILDHOOD ALLERGIES – GENUINE AND, ER, NOT SO GENUINE

GENUINE

Nuts

NOT SO GENUINE

Greens

GENUINE
Milk

NOT SO GENUINE
Washing

GENUINE
Eggs

NOT SO GENUINE
Sitting still for five minutes

PLAYGROUND
POLITICS

If you ever have to drop off or
collect the kids from school,
watch out for the following:

From a certain age children won't
want any overt displays of public
affection in front of their mates –
especially not big, slobbery kisses

Don't try to keep up with the yummy
mummies in the make-up and fashion
stakes – grandparents are happily
excluded from this department!

If you're driving your battered old Morris Minor, park it round the corner so the kids don't die of embarrassment

Don't get into any conversations about holiday plans – camping at Skegness just won't cut the mustard these days

ARE YOU SPOILING THEM TOO MUCH?

They get 'frequent flyer'
discounts to Disneyland Paris

Their nappies have designer labels

They get cheques from the tooth fairy

Their potties have a flush fitted

If any of these apply, then
the answer is yes!

TRAPS TO AVOID

Having your own children so late that
you're a first-time grandparent at 85

Inviting grandchildren for a 'sleepover' –
sleep is the last thing you'll get

Any open-ended invitation to babysit

THINGS GRANDCHILDREN DON'T WANT FOR CHRISTMAS

Anything 'educational'

Sensible clothes

Piano lessons

Pop music CDs chosen by
their grandparents

THINGS PARENTS DON'T WANT YOU TO BUY FOR THEIR KIDS

Anything noisy

Anything that requires half
a dozen batteries

A model aeroplane/boat that
Dad will spend the whole of
Christmas Day assembling

Selection boxes of sweets that will keep
them hyperactive for three days solid

THINGS TO MAKE
THE MOST OF

Those lovely cuddles – they won't be
having any of that when they're teenagers

Rediscovering your inner child as you
play silly games and read stories

The excuse to eat sweets, chocolate and
ice cream because 'they're having them'

Being seen as the fount of all
wisdom and knowledge – they'll
find you out soon enough!

THINGS THE PARENTS DON'T WANT TO HEAR

It was all so much harder in my day…

A word of advice…

Do you realise what it would cost if you had to *pay* for a babysitter?!

You think it's tough now – wait till they're teenagers!

INDISPUTABLE FACTS THE GRANDCHILDREN KNOW ABOUT YOU

You're extremely old (even though you feel in the prime of life)

Any rules imposed at home don't apply at your house

Your house is way too clean and tidy – and that must be remedied immediately

You have a tendency to nod off at any time, which can only be cured by loud screaming and/or jumping on your feet

REALITY **CHECK**

When they tell you that you're the best grandma/grandad in the world, bear in mind that they have very limited knowledge of any of the other two billion grandparents on the planet

When they say they're going to tell you a joke, don't expect it to make any sense

When they say they've made your Christmas present themselves, don't expect an accurate scale model of Windsor Castle or a beautiful hand-stitched bedspread

If they offer you a home-made cake, expect there to be a vital missing ingredient, such as sugar – or cake

THINGS TO LOOK
FORWARD TO

When they get past the messy stage
and your home no longer looks like the
aftermath of an explosion in a biscuit
factory or a Jackson Pollock painting

The time when you're finally relieved
of unpaid babysitting duties

The day when they're old enough to
run errands and dig the garden for you

The day when they finally
invite you round to dinner

If you're interested in finding out more about our books, find us on Facebook at **Summersdale Publishers** and follow us on Twitter at @Summersdale.

www.summersdale.com